GRAFFEX™

DRACULA
BRAM STOKER

ILLUSTRATED BY
PENKO GELEV

RETOLD BY
FIONA MACDONALD

SERIES CREATED AND DESIGNED BY
DAVID SALARIYA

GRAFFEX™

D R A C U L A

Artists: PENKO GELEV
SOTIR GELEV

Editor: Stephen Haynes
Editorial Assistant: Mark Williams

Published in Great Britain in 2007 by
Book House, an imprint of
The Salariya Book Company Ltd
25 Marlborough Place, Brighton, BNI IUB
www.salariya.com
www.book-house.co.uk

ISBN-13: 978-1-905638-52-9 (PB)

SALARIYA

1 3 5 7 9 8 6 4 2

A CIP catalogue record for this book is available
from the British Library.

Printed and bound in China.
Printed on paper from sustainable sources.

Visit our website at **www.book-house.co.uk**
for **free** electronic versions of:
You Wouldn't Want to be an Egyptian Mummy!
You Wouldn't Want to be a Roman Gladiator!
Avoid Joining Shackleton's Polar Expedition!
Avoid Sailing on a 19th-Century Whaling Ship!

Picture credits:
p. 40 TopFoto.co.uk
p. 44 David Salariya
p. 46 © The British Library / HIP / TopFoto.co.uk
p. 47 © 2001 Topham Picturepoint / TopFoto.co.uk
Every effort has been made to trace copyright holders. The Salariya Book Company apologises for any omissions and would be pleased, in such cases, to add an acknowledgement in future editions.

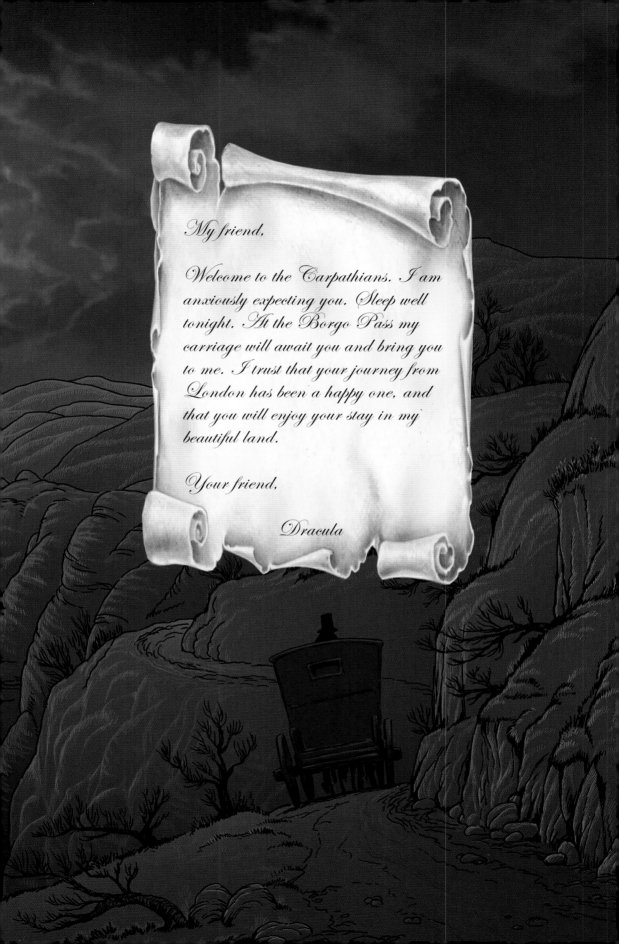

My friend,

Welcome to the Carpathians. I am anxiously expecting you. Sleep well tonight. At the Borgo Pass my carriage will await you and bring you to me. I trust that your journey from London has been a happy one, and that you will enjoy your stay in my beautiful land.

Your friend,

Dracula

CHARACTERS

Count Dracula

Mina Murray (later Harker)

Jonathan Harker

Lucy Westenra

Lucy's mother

Professor Abraham Van Helsing

Quincey Morris

Dr John Seward

Arthur Holmwood

Mr Hawkins

R. M. Renfield

The vampire women

To Transylvania

3 May 1897: Budapest, Hungary

A wonderful place!

Howwwwl!

Jonathan Harker is making his first trip abroad. He's a young English lawyer, on his way to meet a new client – the mysterious Count Dracula. He must travel for days to reach Transylvania,[1] Dracula's wild, remote homeland in the Carpathian Mountains.

Far away from England, Jonathan feels uneasy. He does not sleep well.

Must you go?

Bistritz, Romania

For your mother's sake.

Hell!

Satan!

Witch!

Vampire!

Jonathan reaches a gloomy old inn, where he asks for news of Dracula. The innkeepers shudder and insist on giving him a crucifix.[2] Why?

They hand Jonathan sealed instructions sent by Dracula. He must ride by coach to the Borgo Pass[3] – on St George's Eve, when the local people believe that evil spirits wander. His fellow travellers try to warn Jonathan of the dangers, but he doesn't understand them.

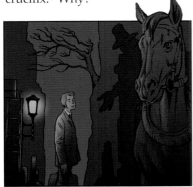

'The dead travel fast.'[4]

It's dark when they reach the pass. A carriage appears at breakneck speed, driven by a tall man with glowing eyes. Jonathan climbs aboard.

As they drive off, wolves snarl around them and eerie blue flames flicker in the darkness.

1. Transylvania: a province of Romania; see map, page 43.
2. crucifix: a figure of Jesus on the Cross, sometimes worn by Christians to protect against evil.
3. pass: a road across high mountains.
4. 'The dead travel fast': Jonathan is remembering a line from a famous German poem.

Dracula's Castle

Welcome to my house! Enter freely and of your own will!

At last, they reach a huge, half-ruined castle, towering on the brink of a precipice. The driver vanishes. The castle seems deserted – but finally Jonathan hears footsteps. Slowly, a locked door opens, with much creaking and groaning.

Let me see to your comfort...

They shake hands, and Jonathan shivers horribly. Dracula's strong grasp is cold and chill – it's like touching a dead man's fingers! Dracula leads the way through dim, cobwebbed halls to a richly furnished chamber.

I trust you will find all you wish.

Jonathan's cold, tired and hungry, so he enjoys the meal that has been prepared for him. But he's surprised to see that Dracula doesn't eat or drink anything.

Listen to them — the children of the night. What music they make!

Wolves howl outside.

Jonathan notices Dracula's hairy palms – and his nails, which are sharp as claws. Nervously, he goes to bed. They have talked so long that it's almost dawn.

Next day, Jonathan sleeps late.

I love the shade and the shadow.

Just after sunset, Dracula arrives. Jonathan asks about the books on the shelves. They're all about England – and they're in English.

Dracula explains why he needs Jonathan's help. He wants to speak English better, and to buy an English mansion.

The house he wants to buy is called Carfax. Jonathan tells him that it is a big, old house, dark and gloomy. Dracula is pleased: a house like this will suit him.

That night, Jonathan can't sleep. He gets up, dresses and shaves before sunrise. Suddenly Dracula appears, looming out of the darkness. But he casts no reflection in Jonathan's shaving mirror!

Jonathan's so startled that he cuts himself with his razor.

Dracula bares his pointed teeth, and seems to want to lick the blood!

Take care! It is more dangerous than you think in this country.

The castle is a prison…

…and I am a prisoner!

But, when he sees the crucifix given to Jonathan by the innkeepers, he stops at once. Angrily, he throws the mirror out of the window.

Once Dracula's gone, Jonathan decides he must find out more about the castle. But his door is locked, and there's a sheer cliff outside the window.

Beautiful and Deadly

Dracula pretends to have servants, yet he does everything himself. Why is he all alone in this ghostly, ghastly castle?

Every night he visits Jonathan and talks about his famous ancestors. Most were warriors – brave and patriotic,[1] but utterly ruthless to their enemies.

Dracula wants Jonathan to stay a month longer in the castle.

He tells Jonathan to write to his employer, Mr Hawkins, to say that he is not coming home yet. Secretly, Jonathan writes to his fiancée, Mina, as well.

Dracula warns Jonathan never to fall asleep in the castle, except in his own room.

Despite his fear, Jonathan's determined to explore. On a bright, moonlit night, he searches for a window from which he can see Dracula's room.

What he sees is unbelievable: Dracula, crawling headfirst down the wall like some huge, loathsome[2] lizard!

1. patriotic: eager to fight for their country against foreign invaders.
2. loathsome: horrible, repulsive.

Forgetting Dracula's warning, Jonathan falls asleep in an empty room. He wakes to see three beautiful women.

They cast no shadows, but move noiselessly in shimmering clouds of moonlight.

One woman glides towards Jonathan, smiling seductively…

…but Dracula storms in, grabs the woman by the throat and drags her away.

He throws the women a sack, which wriggles as if there is a living creature inside it.

The women snatch the sack and paw at it greedily. Then they fade into a cloud of dust in front of Jonathan's astonished eyes, and drift away.

Jonathan faints with shock. He wakes in his own bed. Dracula must have put him there.

DRACULA DISAPPEARS

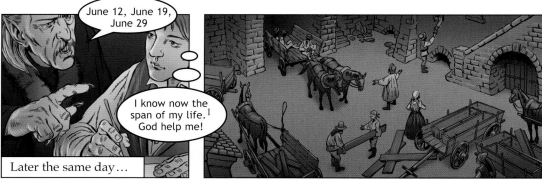

Dracula orders Jonathan to write three letters, dated at different times in the future. All tell Jonathan's friends that he's well.

Jonathan realises that the letters are part of Dracula's evil plan: he wants Jonathan's friends to think he is safe, but then he will kill him. When some Roma[2] arrive to work at the castle, Jonathan asks them to post his secret letter to Mina.

But they are loyal to Dracula, and they hand the letter to him instead. He is furious, and burns the letter.

Soon after, Jonathan finds that all his clothes have vanished from the wardrobe.

The Roma bring large wooden boxes.

Dracula leaves the castle, carrying the sack that he gave to the women. He is disguised in Jonathan's clothes.

A peasant woman hammers at the castle gate, asking for her baby. Dracula summons wild wolves, and they kill her.

The only way Jonathan can get out of his locked room is by climbing out of the window. He's terrified, but he knows he will be killed if he does not escape.

1. the span of my life: how long I have to live.
2. Roma: travelling people.

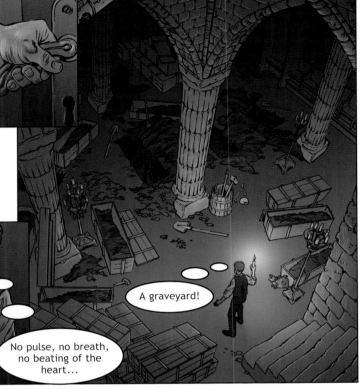

He makes his way through a dark passage to the chapel,[1] where Dracula's famous ancestors are buried.

A graveyard!

He finds the way to Dracula's room and climbs in. It's empty, apart from heaps of gold coins. All of them are 300 years old or more.

No pulse, no breath, no beating of the heart...

Dracula's lying in one of the boxes, on a pile of earth. His eyes are staring wide, his lips blood-red. Is he dead or alive?

There are fifty wooden boxes, and the Roma workmen have been filling them with earth from the chapel floor. What does Dracula need this for? Is it some mysterious part of his plan to move to England?

I must rid the world of such a monster!

Away from this cursed land, where the devil and his children still walk!

Goodbye, Mina!

Dracula must not be allowed to go to England! Jonathan attacks him with the only weapon he can find – but Dracula stirs, and Jonathan loses his nerve.

The workmen arrive to carry the boxes away. Swollen with blood, Dracula is being shipped to England.

Jonathan makes one last attempt to escape by climbing down the wall. He would rather fall to his death than be devoured by those ghostly vampire women.

1. chapel: a Christian church that is part of the castle.

SWEETHEARTS AND FRIENDS

9 May 1897: England

Tell me all the news when you write.

Mina, pray for my happiness!

Schoolteacher Mina Murray is writing to her friend Lucy Westenra. Mina is engaged to marry Jonathan Harker, and tells Lucy of her hopes for a busy, useful future as Jonathan's wife.

Lucy writes back, full of excitement. Three men have asked to marry her, all on the same day!

No... there is someone else...

Won't you just hitch up alongside of me?

Oh, yes!

Oh, Mina, I love him!

The first was John Seward, a hard-working doctor who runs a mental hospital.

The second was Quincey Morris, a brave, adventurous traveller from the USA.

The third was Arthur Holmwood, the son of Lord Godalming. The three men have sworn to remain friends, come what may.

This is a lovely place.

24 July 1897: Whitby[1]

Fool-talk!

Mina and Lucy are on holiday together in Whitby. They stroll in the peaceful churchyard, next to the ancient ruins of Whitby Abbey.

They make friends with an elderly fisherman, and ask him about the local legends. People say that a ghost – a white lady – often appears there.

1. Whitby: a fishing port and holiday resort in North Yorkshire, on the north-east coast of England.

A hundred years is too much for any man to expect.

I wish he were here.

The fisherman says the graveyard is a holy place. He'll soon be lying there himself.

But Mina is worried about Jonathan – she hasn't heard from him for weeks. And now there's another thing to worry about: Lucy has started sleepwalking.

26 July

I do not understand it!

Meanwhile, at Dr Seward's hospital…

This case grows more interesting.

He catches them…

Mr Hawkins has had a letter from Jonathan to say that he's on his way home – but that was a month ago!

One of the patients, Renfield, has started eating small creatures – alive! He puts out sugar to attract flies, spiders and birds.

…crunches them up…

It gives life to me!

…swallows them…

…and keeps a careful note of the numbers.

Dr Seward is puzzled. He decides to study Renfield's strange behaviour. It might help other scientists to understand how the brain works.

THE GREAT STORM

8 August 1897: Whitby is blasted by a terrible storm.

A Russian sailing ship runs aground. There's no sign of life on board, except for a huge dog that leaps ashore and runs away.

Dead!

Once the storm has died down, Whitby sailors explore the wreck. They find the captain at the wheel, clutching a crucifix.

The tale of the ship's log:

There's SOMETHING aboard!

There's not much cargo – just big boxes of earth. But the ship's log-book tells an extraordinary story. After sailing from Varna,[1] the crew complained that an evil presence was haunting them.

Empty as the air!

It IS here! I know it, now!

The weather was awful, and sailors mysteriously vanished in the night. One night, one of the sailors saw a ghostly figure.

The mate[2] attacked it with his knife – but his hand passed straight through! What kind of creature could it be? Mad with fear, the mate jumped overboard.

The sea will save me from HIM!

1. Varna: a Russian port on the Black Sea.
2. mate: second in command

I shall baffle[1] this fiend…

Meanwhile…

Poor dear old man!

By now, only the captain was left alive. He said his prayers, tied his hands to the wheel, and died in the storm.

The old fisherman has been found dead in Whitby churchyard, his neck broken.

Everyone's shocked to see the look of horror on his face – it is as if he had seen Death with his own eyes.

Lucy! Lucy!

11 August 1897

Mina wakes in the night to find Lucy missing. Sleepwalking again! Mina hurries after her. She finds her in the churchyard, stretched out on a tomb – with a ghostly shape bending over her.

Its face is white, its eyes glow red.

When Mina reaches Lucy, the creature has gone. Lucy is clutching her throat, trying to catch her breath. Mina puts her shawl around Lucy's shoulders.

The girls walk home together.

Next day, Lucy says she's fine, but Mina sees two little wounds on her neck. Perhaps Mina pricked her accidentally with the pin of her shawl?

1. baffle: stop, defeat

17

BAD DREAMS, GOOD NEWS

For the next few days, Lucy feels well in the daytime, but anxious and restless at night. She sleepwalks, and gazes out of the window, trying to get out. Mina looks after her carefully.

One night, a huge black bat flutters outside their room. It seems to be calling to Lucy. She gets out of bed and tries to follow it, still sleeping.

Next day, in the churchyard, Lucy spies a tall, foreign-looking figure. She startles Mina – and herself – by seeming to recognise him.

All this time, Lucy has been growing thin and pale, and the wounds on her neck do not seem to be healing.

19 August 1897

News at last! Mina gets a letter from a hospital in Hungary. Jonathan has escaped alive from Dracula's castle…

…but the dreadful things he saw there gave him a dangerous brain fever. He's weak, but getting better. Mina hurries to him.

They get married straight away, without waiting until Jonathan is well enough to travel.

Meanwhile, back in Whitby:

> I am full of life!

At Dr Seward's hospital:

> The Master is at hand.[1]

Lucy's fiancé Arthur arrives to look after her. She feels much better now: she stops sleepwalking, eats much more, and looks pinker, plumper and prettier than ever.

The patient Renfield is behaving very strangely. He's crawling on all fours, sniffing like a dog. He keeps running away to Carfax, a big, empty house nearby which has just been bought by a foreign gentleman.

> I have worshipped you! Now you are near!

Renfield fights the nurses who try to restrain him, but calms down suddenly when he sees a huge bat flying across the moon.

> I shall be patient, Master. It is coming!

He goes quietly back to his room, catching and eating flies as before.

> The blood is the life.

But he still has sudden rages. During one of these he attacks Dr Seward with a sharp knife.

He then tries to lick up the drops of blood from the floor of his cell.

Escaping again to Carfax, he fights with carriers bringing heavy boxes of earth – from the wrecked Russian ship at Whitby!

1. at hand: nearly here.

BLOOD AND GARLIC

24 August 1897

Lucy, now home from her holiday, is ill again. Her neck hurts, and she has nightmares.

She's sleepwalking again, and keeps seeing strange things outside her window. Arthur's alarmed, and calls for his good friend Dr John Seward.

Seward, puzzled, decides to ask his wise old tutor,[1] Professor Abraham Van Helsing. The Professor hurries to help Lucy, all the way from Amsterdam.

At first Van Helsing says Lucy's illness is worrying but not dangerous. But that night she takes a sudden turn for the worse. She has lost blood, and needs an urgent transfusion.[2] Arthur offers to give his blood for Lucy, and she is saved – for now.

Van Helsing is worried about Lucy's neck wounds. He must go home to consult his textbooks.

Seward guards Lucy all through the night. She sleeps peacefully, and looks healthy. But the next night, Lucy sleeps alone…

…and by morning, she is worse than ever. Van Helsing returns, and gives her some of Seward's blood. Again, Lucy recovers.

1. tutor: university teacher.
2. transfusion: blood transfusion was dangerous in the 19th century, because scientists had not yet discovered that different blood groups must not be mixed. It was used only in dire emergencies.

20

These are medicines.

Van Helsing shuts Lucy's window, gives her garlic flowers to wear, and hangs garlic at the window. For a while, Lucy feels better.

The room is awfully stuffy!

But no-one explains to Lucy's mother what the garlic is for! She takes it away and opens the window, thinking that fresh air will be good for Lucy…

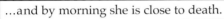

…and by morning she is close to death.

The powers of the devils are against us!

Yet another transfusion is needed, this time from Van Helsing himself.

CRASH!

A few nights later, as Lucy and her mother lie awake, they hear howling all around. Suddenly the bedroom window shatters and the wind rushes in. In the opening, the two women see the head of a great grey wolf.

Alone with the dead! God help me!

Terrified, Lucy's mother clutches at the garlic flowers, tearing them from Lucy's neck. She falls back onto the bed. Lucy realises that her mother has died of fright.

Lucy cannot move, as though she is under a spell. The wolf has gone, and the air is filled with a shimmering, moonlit dust that pours in through the broken window.

Lovely Lucy Dies

"A brave man's blood is the best thing on earth!"

"It is not yet too late. Quick! Quick!"

18 September 1897

Next morning, Seward and Van Helsing fight to save Lucy's life. This time Quincey Morris offers his blood. But where has all the blood gone? Who, or what, is taking it from her?

"She is dying. It will not be long now."

Dr Seward watches over Lucy that night. It seems to him that her teeth look sharper than usual. Once again, a huge bat flaps outside.

In her sleep, Lucy pushes the garlic flowers away.

By morning, her neck wounds have vanished. Van Helsing summons Arthur at once.

"Oh, my love!"

"Not for your life!"

"Grrrr!"

Lucy wakes, and asks Arthur for a farewell kiss. She looks so lovely! He's heartbroken.

But Van Helsing pushes them apart. Lucy is furious! A strange, cruel look comes into her eyes; she snarls like an animal.

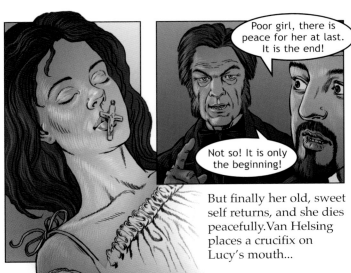

But finally her old, sweet self returns, and she dies peacefully. Van Helsing places a crucifix on Lucy's mouth...

...but in the morning he discovers that the housemaid has stolen it. He says they must now remove Lucy's head and heart. Seward is horrified!

13 September 1897: Exeter [1]

Mina and Jonathan Harker have come back to England, and are busy working together. Mr Hawkins has died, and left them his house and his law business. Jonathan is stronger, but not yet fully recovered.

One day, on a visit to London, Mina sees Jonathan staring at a tall man with red lips and white, pointed teeth. She thinks the man has a cruel expression – but Jonathan seems to recognise him.

Jonathan is shocked, and has to sit down and rest. Mina knows that Jonathan kept a secret diary in Transylvania, and she now decides that she must read it. Once she knows what he's suffered, she may be able to help. She doesn't want him to be ill again.

Back home, they hear the sad news that Lucy and her mother have died. With a sorrowful heart, Mina starts to read Jonathan's diary. It's terrifying!

1. Exeter: the city in the west of England where Jonathan works as a lawyer.

MY GOD! SO SOON!

25 September 1897

Oh, Madam Mina, tell me all that you remember.

I have written it out on the typewriter for you.

Van Helsing visits Mina to ask her about Lucy. She shows him the diary she kept in Whitby. It is in shorthand,[1] which she has learnt to help Jonathan in his work.

Mina also gives him a copy of Jonathan's diary. She does not understand its stories of ghosts, wolves and magic. But Van Helsing tells her that Jonathan isn't mad – all he has written is true!

The visit ends, and Jonathan takes Van Helsing to the railway station. He buys newspapers for the journey.

My God! So soon! So soon!

The headlines are shocking: children in London have been found half-dead, with bites on their necks!

In God's name, Professor, what do you mean?

Van Helsing visits Dr Seward.

Van Helsing says that Lucy has been killed by a blood-sucking creature. Now another such monster is on the prowl…

Those holes in the children's throats were made by Miss Lucy!

…and he thinks it is Lucy! Seward cannot believe this, but Van Helsing says he will prove it.

The bloofer[2] lady…

Together they visit the hospital. The children have bite wounds on their necks, like Lucy's.

1. shorthand: a system of symbols, designed to be much quicker than ordinary handwriting.
2. bloofer: a childish way of saying 'beautiful'.

That night, they go to the London churchyard where Lucy is buried.

What are you going to do?

They find her tomb – but it's empty! This does not surprise Van Helsing, but Seward is horrified.

They go outside, and see a small child in the churchyard. A ghostly figure is bending over it!

Luckily, the child is unharmed.

We were just in time.

See, they are even sharper!

You believe now?

Next day, they go back to Lucy's tomb in daylight. She's back! But her lips are redder than before, and her teeth are like fangs. And, a week after her death, her body is not decaying!

25

UNDEAD!

Van Helsing explains:

She is UNDEAD!

Lucy has been bitten by a vampire – a monster that feeds on the blood of living people. She has become a vampire, too.

The undead are desperate.

Like the ghostly women in Dracula's castle, she is now a hellish, blood-sucking creature.

Is this all a nightmare?

To give Lucy peace, and save her soul, they must kill her once again. Arthur, who was Lucy's fiancé, must give his permission.

This is a mystery…

At midnight they all go together to Lucy's tomb. Once again, they find it empty.

Van Helsing seals the door of the tomb with a paste made from Communion wafer.[1]

Shhh!

They wait, until a ghostly figure appears in the distance. It's Lucy – but looking fierce and cruel, and with a small child in her arms!

Come to me, Arthur. Leave these others and come to me.

Wild and bloodstained, Lucy glides towards Arthur. Her voice is devilishly sweet.

But Van Helsing's crucifix halts her. Lucy's eyes blaze with fury. She spits and growls, viciously.

1. Communion wafer: a special kind of bread used in Christian church services. Evil creatures such as vampires cannot stand it.

Lucy backs away while Van Helsing removes some of the wafer. She slides through the tiny crack…

…and returns to her coffin.

I shall not falter!¹

AAAARGGH!

Now Arthur must act. He hammers a wooden stake through vampire Lucy's heart. She writhes and screams, then grows calm and still. Lucy is no longer a monster – now her soul can go to Heaven.

Arthur kisses Lucy for one last time. Now it's farewell, forever.

There's one more dreadful duty. Van Helsing cuts off Lucy's head, then fills her mouth with garlic and seals the tomb.

One step of our work is done, but there remains a greater task…

Lucy's soul is saved, but Dracula – the vampire who attacked her – is still free. And now he's seeking victims in England. He must be caught and destroyed, somehow!

1. falter: be afraid to do what is necessary.

HUNTING DRACULA

29 September 1897

Mina visits Dr Seward at his hospital. He is reading the typewritten copies of Mina's and Jonathan's diaries.

That is a wonderful machine!

She offers to type out the notes Dr Seward has been keeping. For many months he's been recording his medical reports and private feelings on phonograph[1] cylinders. These notes will help them all to understand the terrible events more clearly.

We have put all the papers in order.

Jonathan and Mina are to stay with Dr Seward at the hospital. They make a list of everything they know so far about Dracula.

Let me be a sister to you in your trouble.

Arthur arrives. He's overcome with grief for his pretty, lively Lucy. Mina does her best to comfort him.

I wish I could comfort all that suffer.

Lucy's death has also made Quincey Morris very unhappy. He says they must work together to track down her killer.

For the blood is the life...

Seward takes Mina to visit his strange patient, Renfield. With Mina, Renfield is quiet and polite, and describes his odd thoughts and feelings calmly.

This vampire which is amongst us is as strong as twenty men.

For the first time, all the friends meet together. Van Helsing explains what vampires are. They have no shadow or reflection, and they sleep in graveyard earth. They can change shape – into wolves or bats, for example – and they grow young again after drinking fresh blood.

28   1. phonograph: a machine for recording sounds on wax cylinders and playing them back.

It is a terrible task that we undertake, for if we fail he must surely win.

We are determined to destroy this monster.

Garlic and crucifixes will stop a vampire. They can't kill in daylight, cross running water, or enter a house uninvited. A stake through the heart will kill them; cutting off the head brings them peace.

Dracula has bought the house at Carfax, close to the hospital.

As they talk, Quincey Morris quietly leaves the room...

BANG!

Eeeek!

He's had 50 boxes of graveyard earth brought there from his castle chapel – by the haunted ship wrecked at Whitby.

As soon as Dracula's full of blood, he'll sleep in one of those boxes until he's ready to attack again.

Sorry!

At the same time:

Let me out of this! Woe is me!

Hear me! Hear me! Let me go!

Quincey had seen a giant bat outside, and tried to shoot it!

Renfield is begging the nurses to set him free. Seward is called to see him. Renfield talks sensibly at first, then becomes frantic.

He says he has an important reason for wanting to be let out, but he will not say what it is. Is it something to do with 'the Master', perhaps?

INVITATION TO KILL

1 October 1897

My friends, we are going into terrible danger!

In manus tuas, Domine![1]

The men arm themselves with knives, guns, wafers, crucifixes and garlic, and go to the chapel at Carfax to hunt for Dracula's boxes. There is a horrible smell of death and decay. But they can find only 29 boxes. What has Dracula done with the others?

It was only the shadows.

They think they see a tall, shadowy figure looming in the doorway – then hundreds of rats squirm all over the chapel floor.

Grrr!

Arthur whistles for his dogs. They are afraid at first, but at last they chase the rats away.

Meanwhile...

I feel strangely sad and low-spirited.

All day, Mina has been looking very tired and pale. She's been crying, which is unusual for her.

She can't forget something that happened the previous night. She couldn't sleep, so she looked out of the window.

A thick mist came creeping into the bedroom – and turned into a tall, ghostly figure with glowing red eyes! Was it a dream?

1. *In manus tuas, Domine*: We put ourselves in your hands, Lord (Latin).

2 October 1897

Meanwhile…

His mood changes so quickly.

Uuurgh!

Later the same night:

Jonathan discovers that Dracula has bought a house in London.

Renfield seems to want to talk about 'souls' and 'blood'. Seward just can't understand him.

Renfield has been fighting, and he's terribly injured. No, worse: he's dying. But how can this have happened? He's been locked in his cell all alone.

I am dying! I have but a few minutes.

Tell us, Mr Renfield.

He beckoned me to the window.

Every one a life! All red blood!

Seward calls for Van Helsing. Renfield must stay alive long enough to explain!

He says he saw Dracula several times, right outside the hospital.

Dracula offered Renfield millions of rats and flies. In return, Renfield promised obedience – and invited Dracula into the hospital.[1]

He had been taking the life out of her!

He raised me up and flung me down.

Tonight, Dracula appeared again, and Renfield attacked him. He realised that Dracula had been trying to prey on Mina, and wanted to stop him. But vampires have superhuman strength, and Renfield was fatally wounded.

---

1. invited Dracula into the hospital: According to legend, vampires cannot enter a place for the first time unless they are invited by someone inside.

BRIDE OF DRACULA!

Van Helsing and the three friends rush to Mina's room. A dreadful sight meets their eyes: Jonathan is unconscious on the bed – and Dracula is attacking Mina!

Dracula has bitten Mina's neck, and now he's forcing her to drink his blood. It trickles from a wound on his chest, and is smeared around Mina's mouth.

Van Helsing springs towards him, with crucifix and wafer. Dracula's mad with rage, but is forced to retreat, growling and snarling.

Quincey Morris and Arthur chase after Dracula. Van Helsing tries to wake Jonathan.

Mina is hysterical, screaming and crying. She he has bite-marks on her neck, just like Lucy's.

Good God, help us!

Dracula's blood has made Mina his slave. He now has the power to control her mind. But Mina says she'd rather die.

Help her! Oh, help her!

Van Helsing says she must not die! Mina must stay alive until they have caught and killed Dracula. Otherwise she herself will turn into a vampire…

Unclean, unclean!

…and have to drink blood, like Lucy.

We have this day to hunt out all his lairs.

By now it's daylight. Van Helsing says they must catch Dracula before nightfall. They'll purify his boxes, so he can't use them to sleep in – all except one box, where they'll trap him and kill him.

If God will let me live, I shall strive to do so.

The men must go out, to hunt Dracula and his boxes, but Mina must rest at home. Bravely she says that she will continue to work – and try to go on living.

Do not fear, my dear.

Mina should be safe. Surely Dracula will not dare attack again before nightfall?

AAARGH!

For extra safety, Van Helsing blesses Mina with a holy wafer. But it burns her flesh, and leaves a sinister blood-red scar!

Could she be turning into a vampire already?

ONE BOX MISSING!

3 October 1897

The men hurry to Carfax chapel and scatter holy wafers in the boxes there. Dracula can't hide in them any more – but he still has his other boxes, all hidden.

They track down most of them in Dracula's new London house and other places in the city.

This place smells so vilely!

By the end of the day they have found all except one. Where can Dracula have hidden this last box? He must have known Van Helsing would be looking for it!

Have all your arms![1]

They go back to wait in Dracula's house. They plan to attack him as he walks in.

At last they hear Dracula coming! His key turns in the lock, and his heavy footsteps get closer. The friends are tense and eager, ready to leap out at him.

GRRRRR!

Alas! Dracula's far too quick and strong for them. He springs away from their outstretched arms and smashes the knives from their hands.

34   1. arms: weapons; also things for their protection, such as crucifixes and garlic.

The friends try to force him into a corner. Dracula backs away from their crucifixes…

…then hurls himself forward and knocks them to the floor. He rushes across the room and leaps through the window.

With a scornful look, Dracula runs away, dropping some of the money he's saved for his escape. Again he's got away from them!

The friends are downhearted. But Van Helsing tells them not to worry: Dracula has left many clues behind. They'll catch him, sooner or later.

They hurry back to Dr Seward's hospital, where Mina is waiting for them. She's still very pale, shocked and sad – but she has an amazing favour to ask them.

Mina begs them to help Dracula's soul find peace, just as they helped her poor friend Lucy. The men all weep. Mina is so kind and forgiving!

READING MINA'S MIND

I have an idea.

Darkness... sailors shouting...

Before they can kill Dracula and give him peace, Van Helsing and his friends must track him down. Mina thinks she may be able to discover where he is hiding.

Ever since Mina drank Dracula's blood, he can 'speak' to her just by thinking. She asks Van Helsing to hypnotise her – he may be able to find out what Dracula is thinking.

Have I been talking in my sleep?

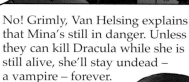

We must find him!

Hearing this dreadful news, Mina faints.

Dracula must be on board a ship. Mina's delighted: surely she'll be safe now, if Dracula has left England?

No! Grimly, Van Helsing explains that Mina's still in danger. Unless they can kill Dracula while she is still alive, she'll stay undead – a vampire – forever.

He is clever, oh so clever!

...with eyes that seemed to be burning...

Urgently, the friends try to find out which ships have just sailed towards Transylvania. Newspapers report that there's only one – the Czarina[1] Catherine.

As fast as they can, they hurry to the London docks. A docker tells them that a tall, pale man boarded the Catherine – taking a big, heavy box as cargo.

1. Czarina (or Tsarina): Empress of Russia.

They also hear that the *Catherine* was late leaving port, because a mysterious fog delayed it. The fog appeared when the captain argued with the tall, pale man…

…but vanished when the big box was loaded. Then the tall man disappeared. The dockers don't know why, but Van Helsing understands: Dracula's on board the *Catherine*, hiding in his last box of earth.

We must get ready!

I must go with you.

The friends must follow Dracula overland to stop him reaching his castle. Van Helsing warns that Mina should not know their plans – Dracula's power over her mind might make her betray them.

Van Helsing sees worrying changes in Mina every day. Her teeth are sharper, her eyes look fierce, her scar will not heal. The men are almost ready to leave when she asks to travel with them.

I swear!

Ashes to ashes, dust to dust…

Mina still needs protection from Dracula's evil power – but she still hopes she can help them. She makes all the men promise to kill her if she starts behaving like a vampire.

Before they leave for Transylvania, Mina asks Jonathan to read the Burial Service[1] to her. For him, it's unbearably sad; but she finds it comforting.

DRACULA'S FINAL JOURNEY

12 October 1897

The Orient Express

They all catch the fast train to Varna, the Russian port on the Black Sea to which Dracula's ship is heading.

The men prepare deadly weapons – guns and sharp knives. Mina's mood keeps changing: sometimes she's restless and alert, sometimes dull and sleepy.

Oh, you so clever lady!

Dracula realises he's being chased, and cuts his mind off from Mina. But she's still able to work out that he's following an ancient route used by his ancestors.

Follow him!

The friends leave the train and split into three groups. Jonathan and Arthur take a steamboat on the river.

Follow!

Seward and Quincey Morris ride on horseback over wild mountains.

Courage, Madam Mina!

Mina and Van Helsing travel by road. Mina now won't eat, sleeps in the day and wakes all night. Van Helsing fears that Dracula will soon totally control her.

4 November 1897

Here you are safe!

They camp near Dracula's castle. Van Helsing surrounds Mina with a circle of holy wafers. She needs special protection against the castle's deadly magic.

Come, sister!

Come to us!

Come!

That night, Mina is visited by the castle's beautiful, blood-sucking women. They call her in sweet voices to join them. Mina is paralysed with horror. Van Helsing's horses die of fright.

"I will go to my terrible work."

5th November 1897

"I hear the howl of wolves."

Leaving Mina safe inside the circle, Van Helsing bravely enters Dracula's castle. Dracula has not yet arrived, and in daylight no-one tries to stop him.

He is looking for the chapel, and the tombs where the three beautiful women sleep during the day.

He hammers a stake through each lovely woman's vampire heart, and cuts off their heads. Magically, their bodies grow old, wither, and crumble.

Meanwhile…

Dracula's box arrives in a Roma wagon. The four friends come galloping after it. They fight, and Quincey is badly wounded.

Dracula's box crashes out of the wagon.

"Look! The curse has passed away!"

They kill him before he can stir. Dracula's evil power has ended. He will never drink blood again! As he dies, Mina sees a look of peace on his face at last – before he crumbles away to dust.

Brave Quincey Morris dies from his wounds. But he dies happy, because the scar on Mina's forehead has finally vanished. She's human again! She's saved!

THE END

Bram (short for Abraham) Stoker was born on 8 November 1847, in Dublin, Ireland. His family was prosperous, comfortable, conventional and middle-class. His father worked as a civil servant for the British government that then ruled Ireland. His mother was well educated, with modern ideas about women's education and careers.

EDUCATION

Bram was the third of seven children. He spent his first years in bed as an invalid. He later said that this made him thoughtful, and helped develop his imagination. But by the age of 7 he was well enough to go to school, where he proved to be a bright, lively pupil. As a teenager, he was keen on sport. In 1864, when he was 17 years old, he went to Dublin University to study mathematics.

Bram enjoyed being a student. He worked hard, but also found time to join the History and Philosophical Societies. He also read novels and poems. His favourites included horror stories, such as *Frankenstein* by Mary Shelley. This was published before Bram was born, but still had the power to shock. He also read sensational poems by early 19th-century 'Romantic' writers such as runaway rebel Percy Bysshe Shelley, 'wicked' Lord Byron and the eccentric Samuel Taylor Coleridge, who was addicted to nightmare-causing painkillers. One of Coleridge's best-known poems, 'La Belle Dame Sans Merci', describes a beautiful woman who might be a vampire.

Bram Stoker

BRAM STOKER THE WRITER

After leaving University, Bram followed his father into a respectable civil-service career. Now he could afford to buy tickets for the theatre, his other great passion. Bram became a lifelong fan of the famous English actor Henry Irving, who often performed in Dublin. He also began to write reviews of plays for the Irish newspapers.

Around this time, Bram made friends with other Irish writers, including the master of horror stories, Sheridan Le Fanu, and Sir William and Lady Wilde, parents of the brilliant but shocking young dramatist Oscar Wilde. Lady Wilde was interested in traditional tales from Ireland and the rest of Europe. These often featured supernatural creatures of various kinds.

A NEW CAREER

At the Wildes' house, Bram met an attractive young woman, Florence Balcombe. They married in 1878, and in the same year they moved to London. Bram hoped to make an exciting new career there. He took the job of Business Manager at the famous Lyceum Theatre, where Henry Irving performed when he was in London. For the next 27 years he worked very hard to manage Irving's theatre business. This often meant leaving his wife and their son (born in 1879) to travel round the world.

HORROR STORIES

Although the theatre kept him very busy, Bram did not make much money. So he tried to earn more by writing. He based his stories on traditional horror tales, but he set them in the modern world. This made them seem more real and shocking. At first Bram's stories were not a success. His writing style was clumsy, and he lacked the insight into human character shown by other, greater writers.

But then, in 1897, Bram Stoker published his fifth novel: *Dracula.* Its exotic setting, brave heroes, wise heroine, glamorous victim – and, above all, its fascinating vampire villain – appealed to many readers. They were also thrilled by his descriptions of the latest scientific developments, especially blood transfusion. Today this is a routine operation, but then it was scary and shocking. But *Dracula* only became world-famous many years later, after the story was filmed.

AFTER *DRACULA*

In 1905, Irving died. The shock almost killed Bram Stoker. He left the theatre, but continued to write stories and newspaper articles. None was as popular as *Dracula.*

Tired and ill, Bram Stoker died in 1912, aged 64.

HAPPILY EVER AFTER…

At the end of *Dracula*, Stoker tells us what happened to his heroes after they defeated the evil Count.

Mina and Jonathan have a son, born on the anniversary of Quincey Morris's death. The boy is named after all the brave friends who shared in their adventure, but they call him Quincey. One summer, they visit Transylvania. The ruined castle is still there, but the evil has gone, as if it had never been.

Arthur Holmwood has inherited the title of Lord Godalming. He is now happily married, and so is Dr Seward.

Professor Van Helsing is very fond of little Quincey. One day, he says, the boy will understand what a courageous woman his mother is, and how many brave men fought to save her.

For centuries, stories about blood-sucking corpses – the living dead – have been told all round the world. At the same time, offerings of fresh blood – the symbol of life and strength – have been made to gods in many different cultures.

In most of these legends, vampires look like humans, but some appear as bats, dogs or spiders. In ancient Indian stories, *vetalas* looked like corpses but hung upside down from graveyard trees. In Middle Eastern myths, *lilu* were beautiful women who killed babies. In China, undead corpse monsters hopped after victims to drain their life-force from them. In Central America, traditional tales described blood-sucking bat-gods. The ancient Greeks believed that the spirits of the dead could be called from their resting place by fresh blood. Roman stories featured the *strix* (screech-owl) – a half-human, half-bird monster that fed on blood from its victims.

Roman monster stories were mixed with stories from Russia, eastern Europe and the Roma people (called 'Szgany' in *Dracula*) to create a long-lasting tradition of vampires. Anything bad that happened – from sickness to wild weather – was blamed on them. The modern word *vampire* comes from a word that means 'witch' in several east-European languages.

East Europeans believed that vampires were ordinary people who had been born cursed, met bad luck, died tragically, or lived bad lives. After death, their task was to spread evil. They had magic powers and could change their shape, especially into wolves. They drank blood and turned their victims into vampires.

Scientific explanations

After about 1700, educated people began to doubt the existence of vampires. They argued that it was stupid and superstitious to believe in monsters. They also suggested scientific reasons why dead bodies change their appearance after death. The flesh of the fingers shrinks back from the nails, making them look longer, like claws. Gums shrink, making teeth look long and fang-like, and gases inside a dead body make it swell, turn blood-red, and – sometimes – twist and turn. Blood or other fluids may trickle from the mouth.

Around 1750, rulers in eastern Europe banned people from digging up dead bodies to look for signs of vampirism. But then writers and scholars began to take an interest in traditional tales. Within 70 years, vampire stories were rediscovered, and became very fashionable, along with other tales of horror and suspense.

Becoming a vampire

According to legend, there are many things that can turn you into a vampire – or make people think you are one – including:

- a physical abnormality, such as an unusually hairy body
- being born prematurely
- dying before baptism
- being the seventh boy or seventh girl in a family
- being looked at by a witch
- your mother being frightened by a black cat before you were born
- committing suicide
- being murdered
- not being buried properly.

PLACES IN THE STORY

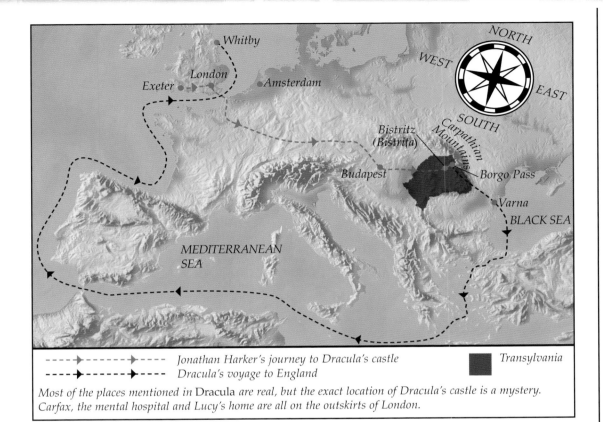

---- ▶ ---- ▶ ---- Jonathan Harker's journey to Dracula's castle
---- ▶ ---- ▶ ---- Dracula's voyage to England

■ Transylvania

Most of the places mentioned in Dracula *are real, but the exact location of Dracula's castle is a mystery. Carfax, the mental hospital and Lucy's home are all on the outskirts of London.*

REAL LIVE VAMPIRES

In the natural world, some parasites (creatures that rely on another living thing for food) survive by sucking blood. They include leeches, ticks, mosquitoes and some species of bat, such as the so-called vampire bat of South and Central America. Many parasites spread dangerous diseases as they bite – for example, mosquitoes can carry malaria. But other parasites can be helpful. Leeches have been used for centuries to suck blood away from wounds, to reduce inflammation and swelling. Some hospitals still make use of them today.

Several plants are parasites, and live by sucking sap from stronger species. The most famous include mistletoe – used for Christmas decorations – and truffles – rare, tasty fungi that grow underground and are highly prized by chefs and gourmets.

A REAL VAMPIRE VILLAIN?

In 1819, John Polidori published the first famous vampire story in English. Called *The Vampyre: A Tale,* it includes a young, innocent hero, two young female victims, and a clever, charming nobleman who proves to be a vampire.

Polidori was the personal doctor of the celebrity poet Lord Byron, and travelled through wild countryside in Europe with him. He based his story on one of Byron's own ideas, and used Byron's character as the basis of his vampire villain.

When writing *Dracula*, Bram Stoker mingled two very different themes: horror stories, often based on traditional tales (below), and new ideas in science, medicine and society (opposite).

1764
Horace Walpole, *The Castle of Otranto* (UK)
Medieval ruins, ghosts, mysteries, an ancient curse and an innocent young person in peril.

1791/2
Christian Heinrich Spiess, *Der Petermannchen* (Germany)
A 'shudder story' – mystery, violence and horror.

1794
Ann Radcliffe, *The Mysteries of Udolpho* (UK)
Wild scenery, exotic locations, young women in danger and a wicked lord.

1796
Matthew Gregory Lewis, *The Monk* (UK)
Ghosts, black magic and devils.

1812–1857
Jakob and Wilhelm Grimm ('the Brothers Grimm') publish their famous collections of German folk tales.

1818
Jane Austen, *Northanger Abbey* (UK)
Makes fun of horror stories – but also includes a scary mystery.

1818
Mary Shelley, *Frankenstein* (UK)
The most famous monster story in the world!

1819
John William Polidori, *The Vampyre: A Tale* (UK)
Based on eastern European legends; scandalous and successful. (See page 43 for more information.)

1820
Charles Maturin, *Melmoth the Wanderer* (UK)
Vampires and an outcast, devilish hero.

1831
Victor Hugo, *Notre-Dame de Paris* (also known as *The Hunchback of Notre Dame*) (France)
Deformity, superstition, a beautiful girl accused of witchcraft – the classic Gothic novel.

1839
Edgar Allen Poe, *The Fall of the House of Usher* (US)
A ruined castle, ancient family secrets, death, decay and madness.

1847
Emily Brontë, *Wuthering Heights* (UK)
Wild country, ghosts, a young girl victim and a mysterious, demonic hero.

1847
Author unknown, *Varney the Vampire* (UK)
A popular, easy-to-read, vampire story.

1848
Charlotte Brontë, *Jane Eyre* (UK)
Brooding hero, innocent young girl, and a madwoman locked in the attic.

1860
Wilkie Collins, *The Woman in White* (UK)
Mystery, magic, disbelief and deception.

1870
Charles Dickens, *The Mystery of Edwin Drood* (UK)
Suspense, disease and death in a big city.

1872
Sheridan Le Fanu, *Carmilla* (Ireland)
A beautiful, deadly female vampire.

1886
Robert Louis Stevenson, *The Strange Case of Dr Jekyll and Mr Hyde* (UK)
Medicine, murder, madness and evil.

1891
Oscar Wilde, *The Picture of Dorian Gray* (Ireland)
Eternal youth, living death, pacts with the Devil.

1891
Sir Arthur Conan Doyle (UK) publishes the first of his Sherlock Holmes stories. Many feature criminal madness.

Garlic is said to keep vampires away.

1837
Isaac Pitman (UK) invents his shorthand writing system.

1842
Anders Retzius (Sweden) suggests that character is shown by shape and size of skull.

1847
Richard March Hoe (US) invents rotary printing press. It prints newspapers cheaply and quickly.

1848
Queens College, London, set up to train women teachers – the first institution to offer academic qualifications to women.

1851
Great Exhibition at Crystal Palace, London. Displays of the latest technology and scientific discoveries from many lands.

1853
Alexander Wood (UK) and Charles Gabriel Pravaz (France) both independently invent the hypodermic syringe.

1859
Charles Darwin (UK) publishes *On the Origin of Species,* suggesting a link between humans and other animals.

1862
Louis Pasteur (France) discovers bacteria – invisible living organisms that can spread from one person to another and cause disease.

1865
Gregor Mendel (Moravia – now part of the Czech Republic) discovers the laws of heredity.

1865
Mathematician Lewis Carroll (UK) publishes a new kind of fantasy novel, *Alice in Wonderland*. Many of its ideas are based on mathematics.

1867
Christopher Sholes (US) invents typewriter with modern 'QWERTY' keyboard.

1874–1880s
Sir William Osler (Canada) and Giulio Bizzozero (Italy) explain how blood clotting works.

1877
Thomas A. Edison (US) invents the phonograph (first sound-recording and playback machine).

1878
Women allowed to study at British universities.

1882
First railway tunnel through the Alps (St Gotthard) links western and eastern Europe.

1885
Louis Pasteur (France) invents vaccine against rabies – a deadly disease passed on by bites from infected people or animals.

1887–1889
Emile Berliner (US) invents gramophone and wax disks for recording sound.

1888
David Gestetner (Hungary / UK) invents duplicating machine.

1892
Thomas Oliver (US) improves typewriter. Now the user can see words as they are typed.

1893
Edvard Munch (Norway) paints *The Scream,* a revolutionary portrait of a disturbed, horrified state of mind.

1893
Valdemar Poulsen (Denmark) invents magnetic sound recorder.

1895
Guglielmo Marconi (Italy) invents wireless telegraph.

1897
Millicent Fawcett (UK) founds National Union of Women's Suffrage Societies, to campaign for women's right to vote.

1900
Karl Landsteiner (Austria) discovers blood groups (varieties of blood that cannot be mixed).

1900
Sigmund Freud (Austria) studies dreams and mental illness.

1901
Elie Metchnikoff (Russia / France) discovers how white blood cells fight infection.

1903
Ivan Pavlov (Russia) explains how reflexes govern human behaviour.

Today, Transylvania is part of the independent nation of Romania. In the past, it was fought over by empires based in Austria, Hungary and Turkey. It is a rugged, mountainous and very beautiful place, popular with tourists; its name means 'The Land Beyond the Forests' in Latin.

In the late 19th century, when *Dracula* was written, Transylvania was poor and undeveloped. It had few cities, roads, railways, or modern inventions such as electric light and telephones. Most Transylvanian people lived as shepherds or peasant farmers; many could not read or write. They did not know about the latest scientific discoveries. Some of them probably still believed in magic – and vampires.

Although *Dracula* contains many pages describing Transylvania, Bram Stoker never visited the country. All his information came from books. He mixed fact and fiction to create his own imaginary version of Transylvania: strange, savage and thrillingly dangerous. The magical, primitive country of Transylvania described in *Dracula* never really existed.

Prince Vlad Dracula (1431–1476); a German woodcut dated 1491

PRINCE VLAD DRACULA

Bram Stoker took the name Dracula from a famous Romanian warrior, Prince Vlad III, who lived nearly 600 years ago. He ruled Wallachia, the area to the south of Transylvania. Vlad's family – like Count Dracula's family in the book – fought to defend Romania from invaders. His father was known as

Dracul ('the Dragon' – but it also means 'the Devil' in Romanian!), because he was a knight of the Order of the Dragon. Vlad III soon became known as Vlad Dracula ('Son of the Dragon'). He was also nicknamed Vlad Țepeș (Vlad the Impaler) because of the ruthless way he executed his enemies. He was a great patriot and fighter, but horribly cruel. He killed many invaders from Turkey and Hungary, but also thousands of Romania's own peasants and nobles. He attacked the Church, and drove foreigners from his lands. But he was NOT a vampire!

Bram Stoker wrote 13 full-length novels (listed below), and many short stories and newspaper articles. He also wrote a handbook for civil-service clerks, and a book in memory of his actor friend and employer, Henry Irving.

1875:	*The Primrose Path*
1890:	*The Snake's Pass*
1895:	*The Watter's Mou'* (The Water's Mouth)
1895:	*The Shoulder of Shasta*
1897:	*Dracula*
1898:	*Miss Betty*
1902:	*A Mystery of the Sea*
1903:	*The Jewel of the Seven Stars*
1905:	*The Gates of Life*
1908:	*Lady Athlyne*
1908:	*Snowbound*
1909:	*The Lady of the Shroud*
1911:	*Lair of the White Worm*

DRACULA MOVIES

The story of Dracula has become one of the post popular subjects for horror-film makers. Over 300 different versions have been produced – though many of them have little to do with Bram Stoker's book. Here are just a few:

1922: *Nosferatu* (Germany)
The first Dracula movie, starring Max Schreck (above). A silent film, made without permission while Bram Stoker's widow was still alive. She won a court case to have it destroyed, but a few copies survived.

1931: *Dracula* (US)
The most famous version, and some say the best. Hungarian Béla Lugosi plays a charming but sinister Dracula.

1958: *Dracula* (UK)
A Hammer Horror classic. Stars British actor Christopher Lee as a cruel, menacing vampire.

1960: *The Brides of Dracula* (US)
Falling in love with Dracula leads to tragedy.

1966: *Dracula, Prince of Darkness* (UK)
A sequel to the 1958 Hammer film; followed by 5 further sequels, 1968–1973.

1975: *The Rocky Horror Picture Show* (US)
A musical comedy sending up vampire movies.

1979: *Nosferatu the Vampyre* (Germany)
A stylish, chilling remake of the first Dracula movie.

1992: *Bram Stoker's Dracula* (US)
Mixes the story of the historical Vlad Dracula with Bram Stoker's novel.

INDEX

FURTHER INFORMATION

IF YOU ENJOYED THIS BOOK, YOU MIGHT LIKE TO TRY
THESE OTHER GRAFFEX TITLES:

Treasure Island by Robert Louis Stevenson, Book House 2006
Oliver Twist by Charles Dickens, Book House 2006
Moby-Dick by Herman Melville, Book House 2007
The Hunchback of Notre Dame by Victor Hugo, Book House 2007
Kidnapped by Robert Louis Stevenson, Book House 2007
Journey to the Centre of the Earth by Jules Verne, Book House 2007
The Man in the Iron Mask by Alexandre Dumas, Book House 2007

FOR MORE INFORMATION ON BRAM STOKER,
COUNT DRACULA AND PRINCE VLAD DRACULA:

www.classic-literature.co.uk/bram-stoker
www.ucs.mun/ca/-emiller
en.wikipedia.org/wiki/Vlad_III_Dracula